CURRENT AFRICAN ISSUES 58

I0122936

Youth and the Labour Market in Liberia

– on history, state structures and spheres of informalities

Emy Lindberg

NORDISKA AFRIKAINSTITUTET, UPPSALA 2014

INDEXING TERMS:
Liberia
Youth
Labour market
Labour mobility
Informal sector
Post-conflict reconstruction
History

ISSN 0280-2171
ISBN 978-91-7106-749-4
© The author and the Nordic Africa Institute
Production: Byrå4
Print on demand, Lightning Source UK Ltd.

Contents

Unemployment and underemployment have big effects on the Liberian economy and are areas of top priority for the Liberian government. Employment is considered "the most urgent demand of the population" (World Bank 2010:1). In Liberia, one third of the population is between 15 and 35 years old (de Mel, Elder et al. 2013:1) and youth make up a large part of the unemployed and underemployed. It has been estimated that about a third of the youths in the Liberian labour force are unemployed (de Mel, Elder et al. 2013:1).[1] Furthermore, 68 percent of the Liberian labour force are employed on the informal labour market (LISGIS 2011:xiii). The International Labour Organization (ILO) finds that the world is currently facing an "unprecedented youth employment crisis" (de Mel, Elder et al. 2013:iii). Together with other international organisations like the United Nations (UN) but also the Liberian state[2], it frequently stresses that unemployed youth can cause instability and conflict. At the same time, youth are also perceived as positive agents for change and for the future. Together, these two discourses make them popular targets for international aid. Youth are therefore a relevant and interesting category to consider in an exploration of the Liberian labour market. This paper asks how is, and has, the Liberian labour market been structured? It pays particular attention to the situation of youth and looks at labour mobilisation and the structure of the informal[3] labour market, both in peace and war. It also examines the idea of unemployed youth as a category of citizens particularly prone to violence.[4]

The paper aims to serve as a background study to future projects on youth and unemployment in Liberia. A recurrent argument is that there are alternative structures of informal governance, referred to as *Big Men* networks, a *Wealth-in-People* system (Bledsoe 1980) or perhaps a *Shadow state*[5] that has co-existed with the formal state since its birth in 1847. These alternative and informal structures entrench society from individual to state level. More importantly for this paper,

1. The definition of youth, used by the ILO Work4Youth report, is based upon the definition used by the Ministry of Labor and the Ministry of Youth and Sport in Liberia (de Mel, Elder et al. 2013:8). Other statistics in this paper, such as LISGIS 2010 refers to 15-24 years of age (LISGIS 2011). The definition of youth, and the fact that an age based definition may be misleading, will be further elaborated upon in section 2.

2. For an example of this, see the National Youth Policy for Liberia (Government of Liberia 2005).

3. The distinction between formal and informal here means that formal is used for "state governed or state controlled, and 'informal' for what is governed by other institutions or partly ungoverned" (Utas 2012a:27).

4. The paper does not consider the link between education and youth unemployment; see de Mel, Elder et al. 2013 for more on this.

5. "'Shadow state' is a concept that explains the relationship between corruption and politics. The shadow state is the product of personal rule, usually constructed behind the façade of de jure state sovereignty" (Reno 2000:45).

they operate on the labour market and are relevant for how labour is being mobilised and jobs are distributed. Perhaps it is wrong to refer to these structures as shadows as this implies illicit activities, when they are actually also a vital and effective part of contemporary Liberia and have many positive and important functions on the labour market (Utas 2008, 2012a, b).

Labour market statistics

To set the scene, recent statistics on the Liberian labour market can help to illustrate the importance of the issue of youth unemployment in Liberia. Both international organisations like the United Nations and the Liberian government have previously referred to an unemployment rate of 75 – 85 percent in Liberia (LISGIS 2011:52, World Bank 2010:8). The Liberia Labor Force Survey 2010 (LLFS) found however that only 7.0 percent of the labour force faces unemployment or underemployment. The unemployment rate alone, according to this research, is 3.7 percent (LISGIS 2011:57). Another recent estimate of the unemployment rate is slightly higher: 5.7 percent (World Bank 2010:1).

A third of the Liberian youths are employed, according to the LLFS, the number being twice as high in rural areas as compared to the cities (LISGIS 2011:31). The unemployment rate among young males is 4 percent, whereas for females it is 8 percent (LISGIS, 2011:52).

The most recent addition to the Liberian youth unemployment statistics comes from the ILO Work4Youth project. It presents different figures compared to the LLFS. According to the Work4Youth report; "one in every three young persons in the labour force is unemployed in Liberia" (2013:1). About half of Liberia's youths are employed, according to this research, but the quality of their work situations is often low (de Mel, Elder et al. 2013:1). Out of the employed, for example, 76.9 percent are self-employed which implies job insecurity (de Mel, Elder et al. 2013:2). The report warns that 78.7 percent of Liberia's working youth fall within the category of underutilised labour, something which creates "a reduced potential tax base, high costs for social assistance and a bottleneck in fuelling the economic transformation of the country [...] [and] can be a source of social instability" (de Mel, Elder et al. 2013:1, underlining added).

Out of the young working population, 80 percent are informally employed and 90 percent face irregular employment. Almost 80 percent of the employed youth receive less than the average wage for all paid workers and self-employed, and the youth seem to find jobs mainly through informal networks (de Mel, Elder et al. 2013:3). Informal work is more common in the rural areas and women work in the informal sector to a larger extent than men (LISGIS 2011:xiii, 66). The United Nations Development Programme (UNDP) estimates that as much as 80 percent of the informal labour market consists of women (UNDP 2013).

It is important to note that developing countries, like Liberia, tend to lack accurate and updated data on their labour markets. Measuring unemployment and formal labour markets in a low-income country with no welfare system – where "very few people can afford to be unemployed" (Cramer 2010:17) – is often unhelpful. The figures presented above can be questioned, and are at times contradictory, but together they point towards the centrality of youth, employ-ment and informal labour markets in Liberia today. As this paper will try to illustrate, it is perhaps the figures on informality and insecure job contexts that better reflect the Liberian reality than strict unemployment rates.

Discourses on youth, unemployment and conflicts

The Liberian state, the UN and other international organisations frequently stress that unemployed youth can cause instability and conflict. The World Development Report 2011 highlights youth unemployment as a main driver of conflict and the most frequently given reason to join rebel movements and criminal gangs (World Bank 2011). The ILO states that "if access to decent work opportunities does not improve for young people [in Liberia] now and in the future, the potential for social and economic instability will increase" (ILO 2009:10).

There is also an academic debate pertaining to this discourse, in which youth have been linked to violence. Collier (2000) and Collier and Hoeffler (2004) argued that a high proportion of young men is an instigating factor for conflict and similarly the *youth bulges* (see Huntington 1996) in contemporary Africa have been used to illustrate a correlation between large populations of youth, economic stagnation and a higher chance of conflict (Urdal 2004). Munive Rincon (2010:195) argues that conceptualising youth as a potential source of violence means adopting discourse on *othering*, where youth become the al-ien other, a "possibly dangerous population that needs help in adapting to the potential that progress brings" (Duffield 2007:9). This discourse is illustrated by the following quote from *the Special Report of the Secretary-General on the United Nations Mission in Liberia*: "the thousands of <u>unemployed youths</u>, ex-combatants, deactivated former soldiers and other retrenched security personnel constitute an incendiary mix of disaffected people with a proclivity to violence that could easily be exploited by spoilers" (UNSC 2009:3, underlining added). Perceiving unemployed youth as a potentially destabilising and violent group in society is arguably a securitisation of employment which renders the group a higher priority with international development agencies (Munive Rincon 2010:195). The Liberian government's focus on the creation of employment for its youth becomes, in line with this argument, pivotal in preventing outbreaks of renewed violence in Liberia. President Ellen Johnson Sirleaf has stated that: "the level of unemployment and the idleness of our youth have a propensity for social disenchantment. For us, employment is synonymous to peace" (Johnson Sirleaf 2006:3).

The paper will further explore the alleged link between unemployed youth and conflict in the case of Liberia. However, it is important to acknowledge that the argument on a causal link between unemployment and violent conflict seems to have little empirical ground. Looking at conflicts all over the world, there are many cases where issues of employment and unemployment have formed part of the beginning and fueling of conflicts. This was also the case in Liberia. Based on available quantitative and qualitative research however, there is no indication of a causal connection between unemployment, employment and wars. Furthermore, there is no evidence on youth unemployment causing violent conflict (Cramer 2010:24).

It could also be argued that the focus on youth as an age-bound category is missing the point. Utas holds that perhaps "it is the number of *social* youth, not the numbers of an age-categorised "youth bulge", that poses a danger for stability in many African countries" (Utas 2012b:1). This perspective perceives youth as a marginalised, "social category of people living in volatile and dire life conditions rather than a group defined by age" (Utas 2012b:1). In this sense it might not be unemployed youth defined by age, but rather unemployment and societal marginalisation as two factors among others that have the potential to stir societal unrest or cause violent conflict. Furthermore, in Liberia, youths are also defined by their lack of integration to, and participation in, the state (Utas 2008:9). Unemployed ex-combatants from the civil wars can serve as an example of this, since they refer to themselves as youths in spite of not always fitting the international age criteria (Utas 2003, 2010). This paper relies on this understanding of youth and perceives it as a fluid social category, predominately inhabited by the young of age.

Another popular discourse emphasises youth as agents for change and stresses their capacity as future stakeholders.[6] Both this discourse and the perception of youth as potentially violent make them a popular target for development aid (Munive Rincon 2010:25, 183–184) and interesting to explore in relation to the Liberian labour market.

A historical perspective and the importance of informal networks

This paper will use a historical perspective in order to understand the structure of the labour market in Liberia and youth's position within it today. Historical structures and functions, as well as the cultural context, of the labour market and labour mobilisation will be explored, considering both peace- and wartime (Cramer, 2008) since they broaden our understanding of, and are recurrent in, the contemporary Liberian labour market.

The patrimonial networks, or the dependence on big men (and big women) structures, dominate the informal labour market and are of particular importance for unemployed youth both historically and today. These patronage networks are traditional modes of governance in Liberia, which Bledsoe has called a

---

6. More on this discourse as well as the discourse on youth as violent see for example de Boeck and Honwana 2004, Abbink and van Kessel 2005 and McEvoy-Levy 2006.

Wealth-in-People system, defining it as essentially " 'being for' someone" (Bledsoe 1990:75, Bledsoe 1980). This means that societal structures are based on the need to have patrons and that the success of someone rests on "the ability to create relationships of obligation and dependency with subordinates" (Bledsoe 1980:55). This system has been part of the distribution of jobs and the labour market as well as the Liberian society at large for a long time. Politically, Liberia declared itself an independent state in 1847 and has since then co-existed with a structure of informal networks operating beside and together with the formal state. These powerful, shadow state networks are sometimes so intertwined with the formal that they are perhaps not best described as shadows (Utas 2008:2). The historical section will illustrate how these informal networks have had great importance for the Liberian labour market in terms of structure and function. As will be demonstrated in the section on the post-war context, many historical structures and forms of labour mobilisation, including distribution of jobs through informal networks, have operated, both in pre-war, war and post-war Liberia.

Pre-colonisation

For nearly 500 years, possibly since the thirteenth century, trade has been common in the Liberian region. Coastal societies in what is now Liberia traded for centuries with Sudanic and Euro-American traders (Handwerker 1974: 232, Handwerker 1980:4–7). European traders would exchange "salt, cloth and guns for gold, cloth dyes, hides, livestock and pepper" (Bledsoe 1980:16) but slave trade became popular as the demand for labour in the American continents increased. At the same time, what is now called Liberia was sparsely inhabited and the inner regions were populated by hunting and gathering groups (Bledsoe 1980:15–16) that engaged in subsistence farming, such as growing cassava and rice. "The family household [was] the most important economic unit" (Liebenow 1969:40–41), but there was also a form of labour cooperative, called "Kuus", where households would work together for increased production. There were several operating markets where tribes exchanged goods with for example Mandingo traders (Liebenow 1960:41,186). During the eighteenth century the trade routes stretched from the savannah to the forest. Some types of trade were based on personal relations between traders and farmers. Other types of trade were controlled and regulated through the local chiefs who in return provided the traders with protection and security (Handwerker 1980:6–9).

Colonisation and independence

In 1822, Liberia was founded by the American Colonization Society (ACS). The colonisers were composed of "free people of African descent, freed slaves, and Africans taken from impounded slave ships" (Abramovitz and Moran 2012:123–124). The settlers, called Americo-Liberians, settled along the coast lines of the territory whilst the ethnically diverse and loosely organised indigenous communities were, to a certain extent, left to continue their lives in the hinterland. The ACS and the Americo-Liberians nevertheless claimed ownership of land in the hinterland. Traditionally, land tenure in Liberia was "based upon the use rather than ownership through purchase" (Liebenow 1969:25). Most of the Americo-Liberians were not interested in farming, something which they associated with life as a servant or slave (Liebenow 1969:12). Instead they came to run farms from a distance. At these farms indigenous labour was exploited and; "the outrageous wage differentials, the lack of amenities, the unregulated power of farmers to 'fine' their employees and the abuses of the apprenticeship system under which young natives were assigned to Americo-Liberian families until they came of age created a situation in Africa not unlike the very one against which the repatriated Americo-Liberians had rebelled in America" (Liebenow 1969:25).

Until 1841, the settlements were governed by American governors appointed in America by the ACS. The governors were assisted by a legislative council which was elected by the colonisers, the Americo-Liberians, and local officials. Nevertheless, Liberia was governed from Washington D.C. where a board of managers had the final say on laws that were passed. In 1841, the last white governor, Thomas Buchanan, was replaced by the settler Joseph J. Roberts and in 1847, Liberia declared independence (Akpan 1973:218).

The population of the new republic was divided, geographically, culturally and politically. The Americo-Liberians kept American traditions in terms of housing, food customs and clothes. They spoke a different language, had a different religion – the Americo-Liberians were Christians whereas the indigenous peoples were predominately Animists or Muslims – and their societal structures were different. The indigenous communities were structured into villages where local chiefs or elders governed. There were also secret societies like the female *Sande* and the male *Poro* which served important, social, political and economic roles (Akpan 1973:219–224).

From the end of the 1850s, the Americo-Liberians began to expand their sphere of influence from their base in Monrovia into the Hinterland, lured by the abundance of natural resources and potential export products such as gold, ivory and camwood (Akpan 1973:222). Americo-Liberian traders "gradually displaced the Mandingoes and even the European merchants and monopolised the trade between the coast and the interior" (Liebenow 1969:14).

The Liberian government was weak due to its smallness and limited capacity. Demographically, the hinterland peoples of sixteen or more indigenous groups outnumbered by far the Americo-Liberians (Liebenow 1969:17), and were in general left to continue their traditional ways of governing (Akpan 1973:222–223). The division between the formal "Western" state and the "alternative", informal patrimonial networks, that in contemporary Liberia operate in parallel but are also intertwined, could perhaps be traced back to this time as a point of origin.

It was in 1898 that President James Coleman first made more determined attempts to take control over the inner regions, called the hinterland, both through more peaceful means and by the use of force. None of these methods were initially supported by neither the Americo-Liberians nor the hinterland peoples, but Coleman's efforts for integration and expansion of the state was continued by coming presidents (Azevedo 1969:46, Akingbade 1994:277–278).

During the period of colonisation and the first years of the new republic, there were many violent protests from groups in the hinterland including the Gola, Grebo and Kru tribes (Liebenow 1969:21). Opposition to the Americo-Liberians also came from European slave traders as well as the British and the French in neighbouring countries, who encouraged groups like the Gola and Bassa to attack (Liebenow 1969: 21–22).

The 20th century

During the 20th century, the Liberian labour market was created following the introduction of industrial technologies. It was marked by exploitation, informality and patrimonial structures. Power and wealth were centralised into the hands of the presidents and their closest collaborators, the Americo-Liberian elite and international companies like the American Firestone rubber company. Liberian youths, predominately men, were the "backbone of the labour force" (Utas 2010:116). After independence, young males found employment but also forced labour in the Americo-Liberian coastal centres, working in the trade and shipping business for example. As the Liberian state begun to consolidate, youth were employed within the army and when the resource extraction economy developed, employment possibilities were found on the large plantations (Utas 2010:116).

The system of indirect rule

In 1904, Arthur Barclay (1904–1912) became the president of Liberia. Barclay imposed a system of indirect rule inspired by the British colonial system of government (Ellis 2007:42). The territory was divided into administrative districts over which commissioners, mainly Americo-Liberians, were appointed. The commissioners cooperated with the local chiefs who in their turn collected taxes and recruited labour for the state (Akingbade 1994:292). Many local chiefs found this an acceptable arrangement since their authority was still recognised (Azevedo 1969:47), but it was also perceived as colonisation rather than integration into Liberian society by the indigenous peoples (Akingbade 1994:280–281). The new administrative system and its hierarchical structure helped the Liberian state to "build and sustain a vast and loyal patronage network in the hinterland" (Levitt 2004:139). The government also created markets that were formed around the administrative centres. In the 1920s, these markets mainly served political purposes, as venues for communication between the government and the hinterland, but they also functioned as a way to increase control over interior trade routes, previously in the hands of local big men (Handwerker 1974:17–18). Even though the system of indirect rule was appreciated by some local chiefs, it also proved effective for assuring governmental control over local structures. The district commissioners supervised the local chiefs and came to control "progressively greater resources of political patronage. Indirect rule became a source of revenue, and the interior a reserve of wealth for Liberian officialdom, from which the great majority of the indigenous population gained little" (Ellis 2007:42, see also Akingbade 1997:262). The officials working in the districts were underpaid but with the help of the Frontier Force, established in 1908, they could collect taxes in an often brutal way (Akingbade 1997:264).

The Frontier Force and forced labour

The Liberian Frontier Force was established in 1908 to impose control over the hinterland. The Frontier Force recruited individuals from different indigenous groups in order to integrate them into the state structure (Akingbade 1994:284 Levitt 2004:146). It was created to help consolidate state sovereignty but this proved a challenging goal as the hinterland peoples protested and the Frontier Force became involved in several battles with different indigenous groups (Utas 2009:277). One of the Frontier Force's tasks was to collect tax, for example the "hut tax", imposed in 1916. Intended to help in financing the construction and running of schools and hospitals, the hut tax generally ended up in the pockets of the elites (Akpan 1973:230, Akingbade 1994:283–284).

Charles DB King's (1920–1930) hinterland policy has been called "an iron hand in a velvet glove" (Akpan 1973:234) On the one hand, King traveled to the interior regions to listen to grievances and installed a programme for elementary education in the hinterland. On the other hand, foreign visitors reported slave-like labour conditions. In 1921, the government initiated a project to build roads in the interior. The hinterland population was forced to carry out unpaid construction work and the local chiefs who did not collaborate were punished. Illegal fees and fines were also levied, often with the brutal assistance of the Frontier Force. The Frontier Force further aided Americo-Liberian contractors in the recruitment of labourers for work on plantations and in mines. Indigenous people were also shipped off to Spanish plantations to work for little or no money (Akpan 1973:231–234, see also Akingbade 1997).

In 1927, international criticism of the Liberian government's labour policies was growing. President King was forced to accept an investigation by a League of Nations commission of inquiry (Azevedo 1969:56). The commission found evidence "of a series of high crimes resembling slavery, forced labour, pawning, abuses of contract labour sent to Fernando Po, and forced labour without the payment of wages" and that the Frontier Force had been assisting in this (Akingbade 1997:270–271). International criticism followed, eventually leading to King's resignation in 1930. The following president, Edwin J. Barclay (1931–1943), imposed several reforms but only made superficial changes when it came to the reasons for accusations of slavery (Akpan 1973:234). The League of Nations launched a Plan of Assistance but when Liberia's economy began to flourish in the 1930s and World War II became the main focus for the coming years, it was never implemented (Akingbade 1997:273). However, forced labour recruitment through local chiefs, to companies like Firestone or the Liberian-American-Swedish Conglomerate (LAMCO) which extracted iron ore, was reported as late as well into the 1950s (Munive, 2011:65).

Firestone

Invited in 1926 by the King government to extract rubber in exchange for revenues to the state, Firestone soon controlled the larger part of Liberian rubber extraction (Munive 2011:361–362). The government confiscated land that had been cultivated by the indigenous peoples and sold much of this to Firestone and other foreign companies to use for plantations. Both Firestone and the government were in need of hinterland labour; the government for building roads, and Firestone for work on the plantations. Like the government, Firestone collaborated with the local chiefs and the district commissioners to draft workers (Knoll, 1991:60–67). The labourers on the Firestone plantations and other private plantations were mostly paid a low wage (Munive Rincon 2010:61), but, as noted above, forced labour was a frequent feature, at least in the early years (Liebenow 1969:67).

Tubman – foreign domination of the economy and patrimonial rule

The collaboration between Firestone and the government is the best example of the foreign domination of the Liberian economy. The Open Door Policy, introduced in William Tubman's (1944–1971) first year as president, further opened up Liberia to foreign companies. The Americo-Liberian wealth and the economy of Liberia was, apart from being based on the involuntary labour and marginal wages of the indigenous population, also dependent on external sources such as missionary funds, foreign aid programmes and the American government. As a result of the Open Door Policy and the involvement of international economy, the economy developed quickly:

> "[T]he capital and managerial skill required to exploit Liberia's agricultural and mineral resources [was] secured from foreign sources, with Firestone Plantations and the various mining and other concessions owned and operated by Americans, Germans, Scandinavians, Swiss, and other non-Liberians. The merchandising of commodities [was] largely in the hands of Lebanese and Syrians. Even the large rubber and fruit plantations owned by the Americo-Liberian elite [were] in many cases managed by West Indians, Sierra Leoneans, and other non-Liberian[…][s]" (Liebenow 1969:94).

Tubman delegated all offices of importance through patrimonial relations and many of his allies, including former presidents and political colleagues, could be found on the boards of the concessions, or running large-scale farms (Liebenow 1969:93–94)

Tubman's policies nevertheless had their benefits: "the growth of political patronage and the creation of a national labour market to provide workers for the Firestone plantation or some other foreign concession or for the plantations owned by the wealthier members of the Amercio-Liberian elite, meant that the recruitment of forced labourers became less harsh. People began to work for salaries voluntarily" (Ellis 2007:48–49). In a way, it also weakened the Wealth-in-People system, providing youth with the possibility of social climbing (Ellis 2007:49, see Bledsoe 1980). In reality however, the Wealth-in-People system did not disappear, it was rather one type of big men that came to be replaced by another. In the early 1960s for example, indigenous labourers expressed a preference for working on private America-Liberian plantations instead of the large concessions like Firestone. This was because the private employers often served similar functions as local chiefs traditionally did, attending to financial difficulties and family disagreements for example (Clower et al. 1966:330–331, see also Munive Rincon 2010:64). Bledsoe argues that the programmes to expand infrastructure facilitated migration to urban areas like Monrovia where it was possible to work for a wage and improve one's prospects (Bledsoe 1980:21–22).

Tubman also imposed the Unification Policy which was an attempt to make Liberian culture and traditions more important, and increase political equality (Akpan 1973:234). In 1954, Tubman created four new counties in the hinterland. These reforms gave many indigenous Liberians "a genuine stake in the republic and the body politic" for the first time (Levitt 2004:187). Tubman also included hinterland people in his government. He established a national school system that was no longer only reserved for the America-Liberian children (Bledsoe 1980:22–23). The policies for an integration of the hinterland peoples and the establishment of schools for all, created a countryside elite of youth who demanded employment in the state structure and inclusion into the state (Ellis 2007:49, Sawyer 2005:16).

Tubman served as president for 27 years and managed to transform "the presidency into a personal cult" (Sawyer 2005:16). Apart from the reforms imposed, Tubman also formalised the big man system creating a:

> new political base of settlers of low status, indigenous chiefs, and members of the Monrovia elite who had become greatly disaffected with their own inner circle. He doled out public monies to buy loyalty, established and elaborated a greatly feared security network, crushed those members of the opposition whose loyalty he could not buy, and rammed through legislation and a constitutional amendment removing presidential term limits (Sawyer 2005:16).

Young men and waged labour

In the 1950s, the Liberian economy prospered (Ellis 2007:49). The export of iron and rubber had greatly increased and many new foreign concessions had been established (Bledsoe 1980:21). In 1970, "every eleventh Liberian worker out of a total of some 105,000 in the money economy got a job in a mining industry" (Schulze 1973:163), and at least 43,000 wage workers were found in the rubber industry (Schulze 1973:113).

The labour market was essentially created and modeled to benefit the developing resource-extraction economy (Munive 2011:357), as exemplified through the recruitment strategies of companies like Firestone. Another example of employment in the resource extraction economy was the Bong Mine in Fuama Chiefdom. Reminiscent of today where young men go to work in mines or on plantations (see the post-war section), the Bong Mine attracted "young men to work for money – mostly residents are immigrants – and it attracts people who live off the young men who make the money" – indicating the potential for business surrounding this group – including for example shop owners and prostitutes (Bledsoe 1980:38). This type of contract labour created new migration patterns where young men left their home villages to look for work. This in its turn resulted in a countryside "increasingly dependent on remittances from migrants" (Utas 2010:116), which is also, in many ways, still the case (see the section on remittances).

Beside the work on plantations and in mines, there was also an increasing amount of job opportunities within the state bureaucracy and other formal work, which provided possibilities for young and educated men to enter into waged employment. However, "the 1962 census revealed that only 3.4 percent of the population (including expatriates) was employed in skilled professional, technical, administrative, or clerical jobs" (Bledsoe 1980:20). Men without the skills required for these types of jobs and who did not go to work at the concessions or in the mines, became for example tailors, drivers or carpenters. There were also many men and women who, in order to access money which was becoming the dominant means of exchange and to be able to remain in the urban areas, began to trade. This led to a huge increase in the number of marketplaces between 1950 and 1970 (Handwerker 1974: 231–234). The following example mirrors in many ways the underemployed or informally employed youth described in the post-war section:

> This is the background of the men sitting along the sidewalks of Waterside in Monrovia waiting to be hired to carry some small thing a short distance; the peddlers with their "tables" of assorted candies, gum, biscuits, cigarettes, and matches; the "Yannah boys" traveling around Monrovia with stacks of brightly colored "Fanti" cloth (imports from Netherlands, France, and Japan); and most of the market sellers in Monrovia who deal in imported cloth, household wares, and such (Handwerker 1974:233–234).

Women entering the (informal) labour market

The main participants of the emerging market system were women. Traditionally, the activities of Liberian women were located in and around the home, but when many Liberian men entered into waged labour, women's responsibility for household subsistence and finances grew. In urban areas, like Monrovia, the jobs available for men were often temporary and contract based. There were often large periods when the male members of a household were unemployed. These factors made women start to trade. Other reasons given were for example "to help their husbands, to earn money for themselves not provided by males, and to avoid having to rely on their kin for money" (Handwerker 1974:239). There were also alternative forms of employment available for women in the cities such as "housecleaning, babysitting [and work as] cooks" (Handwerker 1974:241). Bledsoe found that among the Kpelle in Fuama kingdom, women in urban areas had better chances of finding paid work as compared to women in rural areas (Bledsoe 1980:117). Bledsoe also noted that working women still tried to "maintain strong bonds with their children and other people in their household, creating ties of debt and obligation with dependents whose labour and earnings they seek" (Ibid). This illustrates how the Wealth-in-People system operated within households, in this case for women in their quest for *Big Womanity* as part of their intra-household strategies for survival.[7]

The Liberian army and unemployed urban youth

In 1956, the Liberian army replaced the Frontier Force. It consisted to a large extent of hinterland youths that were recruited through patron-client networks, where local chiefs and villages supplied recruits to the government. Being a soldier was a way to climb the social ladder and upon returning home, soldiers would receive a higher status, taking their seat among the elders and chiefs of their villages. With the expansion of industrial technologies and the increasing demands for political inclusion, "the security challenges facing the Liberian government could no longer be effectively handled by a patrimonial military force" (Sawyer 2005:24). In the late 1960s, a national military academy was established and the system with local chiefs as recruiters ceased. Instead the Liberian government began to recruit "heavily from among the growing pool of unemployed and unskilled literate and semiliterate young men of urban and peri-urban communities in the hope of both building a professional military and reducing urban unemployment" (Sawyer 2005:24).

Increasing instability

A longer period of peace and stability came to an end in the late 1970s. William Tolbert, (1971–1980) who became president in 1971, had previously served

---

7. In relation to this section, Abramovitz and Moran interestingly point out that rural women and women of Americo-Liberian descent had very different opportunities to enter the labour market. Traditionally, rural women engaged in subsistence agriculture and served as the breadwinners for the family. Although not being considered "equal" to men, these women were less dependent on their husbands than urban, educated Americo-Liberian women who faced more constraints pertaining to a culture with a traditional western understanding of gender relations. An Americo-Liberian woman was for example generally expected to be economically dependent on her husband and stay at home (Abramovitz and Moran 2012:124–125).

as vice-president under Tubman for almost 20 years. Aiming to carve out his own niche of power, Tolbert continued to centre the power on himself and a loyal network. At the same time, the president could not ignore the new social category of well-educated youth that demanded political reform and inclusion as well as the Liberians who had disliked Tubman – the settler intelligentsia, military elite, university professors and other groups (Levitt 2004: 191–192, Ellis 2007:50). In response, Tolbert developed the infrastructure and expanded the education and health care systems. Many educated youths from the hinerland were given jobs within the state structure (Sawyer 2005:16). These reforms, nonetheless, made him unpopular with the conservatives of his own party, the True Whig Party (Ellis 2007:50).

The Liberian economy was declining and "[y]oung men [that] had earlier been able to rely on the income generation of a few years' work on plantations – or similar forms of employment – in order to establish themselves in their home villages by investing their saved income, as well as their 'modern' social capital, in a farm, a house, wife (or wives) and family […] [found it] increasingly difficult to obtain funds and the benefits that followed. They were thus forced, over extended periods of time, to survive on underpaid contracts in towns and plantations" (Utas, 2010:116). This also added to the societal unrest and is notably a pattern that is recurrent in contemporary Liberia (see the post-war section).

In the end, the Tolbert government did not succeed in meeting the demands of the Liberian population. This coincided with falling commodity prices. In an effort at inclusion and distribution of more jobs, Tolbert further expanded the Liberian armed forces and the government recruited from the cities in an attempt to reduce urban criminality (Munive Rincon, 2010: 71–72). Nevertheless, in 1979, the already weak government faced additional instability. An increase in the price of rice, the staple food, led to public uproar and riots in Monrovia. The general perception of the public was that this only benefitted a small elite in which Tolbert, who made money out of rice production, and his loyal network were included (Munive 2010:71–72).

Samuel Doe

In 1980, Tolbert was overthrown by a military coup executed by young junior officers of the Armed Forces of Liberia headed by Sergeant Samuel K. Doe. Doe's political agenda aimed at inclusion of the hinterland peoples, finding support and legitimacy in grievances, based on ethnicity and rural marginalisation (Munive 2011:366–367, Bøås and Dunn 2013:35). He was the first indigenous Liberian president but this interlude was brief as both Taylor and now Ellen Johnson Sirleaf are partly of Americo-Liberian descent and closely connected to Americo-Liberian elites (Utas 2008:7). Doe's People's Redemption Council (PRC) enjoyed broad-based support at the start but came to play on ethnic cleavages as well as reinforcing the patrimonial system in favor of the president. High-ranking military positions were given to those who belonged to Doe's own ethnic group, the Krahns, as well as the Mandingoes, while the Gios and Manos of Nimba County, two other dominant ethnicities in Liberia, were scapegoated and excluded from political society (Ellis 2007:65, Utas 2009). It was nevertheless a case of one elite and one hierarchy being replaced by another (Moran 2006:98). During the Doe regime, the plantation economy and dependence on foreign concessions continued. Doe "continued to work his patronage system with impunity, like his True Whig predecessors, by granting concessions to foreign businessmen who were beholden to him for commercial opportunities and by taking bribes from them with which to buy local political support" (Ellis 2007:64). Doe's regime was supported by the United States and other external actors since Liberia "was considered to be of strategic importance in the global security arrangements of the Cold War" (Sawyer 2005:20). For example, Liberia received a large package of American military aid, which Doe came to use for his own protection against other "ambitious young Master Sergeants" (Moran 2012:56) who were looking to replace him. After the presidential elections in 1985, which Doe claimed to have won by 51 percent while there was ample evidence of it being fraudelent, violence and dissent were stirring (Moran 2012:56).

The Civil Wars

In December 1989, a military group later known as the National Patriotic Front of Liberia (NPFL) invaded Liberia. This group quickly disintegrated into two factions, one led by Prince Johnson and one by Charles Taylor. This was the onset of over ten years of violent conflict, involving the rebel movement United Liberation Movement for Democracy in Liberia (ULIMO) that later became the ULIMO-K and ULIMO-J, and many other actors (Specht 2006:15, Utas 2005a:55). The rebel movements of the Liberian civil wars were financed similarly to how the Liberian state, and its shadow structures, had been financed prior to the war. The importance of sponsorship from foreign states continued from pre-war to war. Furthermore, "rebel leaders built up ties with commercial foreign interests as a way to finance their movement, strengthen their position relative to rivals, and provide resources for developing a cadre of clients and followers" (Murphy 2003:71). Adding to this, Utas notes that: "informal wartime networks consist of a multitude of actors: politicians and political parties, military, finance, NGOs, national and international actors, religious leaders, businessmen, warlords and trade union leaders" (Utas 2012a:17).

The first part of the civil war ended in 1996 when peace talks were held, resulting in the Abuja Peace Accord and a formal ceasefire. Taylor won the following general election in 1997. Like the previous presidents, he steered power to himself. Taylor also used the formal state structure for shadowy illegal and criminal activities, including illicit economic transactions and the extraction of resources (Sawyer 2005:38). Violent conflict erupted once more in 1999 when another armed movement, opposing Taylor's government, the Liberians United for Reconciliation and Democracy (LURD) invaded from Guinea. In 2003, Taylor resigned and was replaced by a transitional government and in 2005, Ellen Johnson Sirleaf, the current president, was elected.

"The labour force of war"

The Liberian civil wars have been referred to as "a crisis of youth" (Richards 1995) indicating one of its most central group of actors. Marginalised and unemployed youth were mobilised to fight through similar patrimonial networks that had previously been activated for the recruitment into the military and other types of labour arrangements involving Big Men structures (Munive Rincon 2010:52,79). Even though the elites essentially remained the same, similarly to earlier changes in society, war made it possible for youth to change their position in it (Utas 2013b, see also Utas 2003:231). In making their own fortune through participation in violent conflict, young men (and women) could, if successful, become big (wo)men.

Young women were also mobilised as fighters. There were, for example, female commandos such as the Women's Artillery Commandos (WACs) within the LURD (Specht, 2006:15). Other young females turned war into good business (Utas, 2005:74). Looking at the first part of the civil wars, Coulter et al., argue however, that even though women were able to advance in society during wartime, the majority of the young women nevertheless found themselves in similar positions after the war had ended as when it begun (Coulter et al., 2008:17, see also Utas 2005a). It is important to add that "the labour force of war" (Cramer 2008:122) or "the war machine" (Hoffman, 2011a) also included other tasks resembling professions, for example spies, cooks and paramedics (Specht 2006:20–24).

Even if it was a war of youth, it was not directly sought after by youth. It nonetheless became however; "an opportunity to obtain what many youths had failed to access through their initial migration from countryside to city or plantation. Economic prosperity and the sensation of power once again connected young men to the dreams of the modern world of goods and money" (Utas, 2010:117, see also Utas 2013b). One reason for fighting was unemployment, but it was one of many (see for example Pugel 2007). A large pool of people was available for work as combatants due to their societal marginalisation, or perhaps because participating in one way or another, was the only rational option in the midst of civil war. Unemployed youth should not be perceived as the sole, or major, cause of the conflict. Rather, as this historical account has illustrated, there are many intertwined factors such as inequality, political misruling, political and economic exclusion – essentially the failure of the Liberian state to deliver basic services and security to its citizens that together form the background of the many years of violent conflict in Liberia.

This section predominantly focuses on male ex-combatants, but also youths in general, and shows that historical structures for labour mobilisation have continued from the pre-war to the post-war. War has also, as will be demonstrated, had effects on the Liberian labour market. It is important though to note that war does not necessarily make things go backwards, meaning that war is not simply "development in reverse", as Collier famously claimed (Collier 2003:33).

Ex-military networks

In post-war Liberia, networks from the civil wars continue to operate as young men often depend on military structures for work opportunities. This could for example be observed in the DDRR process. With its promise of access to financing, education and vocational training, the process was not only attractive to former combatants but also to those who had not participated in the fighting during the wars. In the end, over 100,000 people went through DDRR and a large part were not ex-combatants. Patrimonial networks were effectively reinforced and expanded in this process as military commanders were appointed as gatekeepers, controlling who would get access to the programme (Hoffman 2011a, Munive 2011:372).

Today, former commanders can still play an important role in finding, mobilising and distributing labour in the face of unemployment, similarly to the historical roles of local chiefs and other big men. Findings by Themnér and Utas suggest that former commanders are good managers who "know how to organise people and maintain respect and loyalty over workers" (Utas 2013b). The networks over which they preside are also useful to politicians and business-men in need of labour and/or political support (Utas 2013a). Through ties with their former commanders, some ex-fighters are made accessible for sudden work opportunities, in Monrovia or elsewhere in Liberia (Hoffman 2011a, 2011b). Hoffman calls this "just-in-time" production and argues that it is the same men and networks that could be deployed for work on the battlefield as on the plantations or in the mines (Hoffman 2011b:42, see also Munive 2011:228). These types of informal networks, in Liberia and also in neighbouring Sierra Leone, were indeed used in Côte d'Ivoire in 2011 or for overseas security work in Iraq (Utas 2013b, reference to Mynster Christensen 2013). Nevertheless, they have also been used to create stability (Utas 2013b). Utas found in his fieldwork in Nimba County that former generals have "in fact aided their former soldiers to reintegrate into formal livelihoods and civilian lives" (Utas 2013a). Käihkö, on the other hand, argues that the idea of ex-military networks is perhaps losing relevance, since informal networks are usually mixed, including also family members, friends and colleagues (Käihkö 2014).

Liberian youth – a *population flottante*?

"Anyone who needs fifty workers for their rubber plantation, or 150 persons for a demonstration can approach these brokers", writes Utas (2013b), referring to ex-commanders and their informal networks of ex-soldiers and unemployed, or perhaps better termed underemployed and underutilised, youth. As discussed in the previous section, Hoffman argues that there is a young and mobile workforce in Liberia today, reminiscent of the one described in the 1970s, consisting of male ex-combatants, and arguably other youths, that concentrate in large groups attracted by the opportunitiesof urban areas like Monrovia. Mobilised through informal networks, they can be quickly gathered and deployed for different types of work at different sites (Hoffman 2011a:164). These large pools of youth have been referred to as a *population flottante* (Hoffman 2011a:14,188). Hoffman also uses the idea of the city as "barracks" in order to illustrate how rural youth migrate to urban areas to find employment, and take on day-to-day jobs, sometimes only to return to work in the countryside – in plantations and mines for example – or perhaps are deployed for violent labour (Hoffman 2007, see also Utas 2012:3). Themnér similarly found in his fieldwork that young men tend to gather in the city and then go off to work in rural areas – in mines or on plantations – since that is where the money is. They then return to the city and invest their incomes in a continued life there (Themnér 2013). In one sense, this *population flottante* is not able to settle down. Similarly to the Liberian men who entered waged labour in the middle of the last century, these men seem to be predominantly employed in temporary, contract-based work that generates long periods of unemployment. This could make them a potentially destabilising factor in society.

Agriculture and the appeal of urban modernity – what jobs do youth desire?

The Liberian economy is vulnerable and depends on its export of commodities and is determined by international demand. Making agriculture, which forms a large part of the informal economy[8] and includes many smallholders and subsistence farmers, more market-oriented and integrated with the formal exports-oriented economy could create more employment possibilities (Eriksson Skoog 2009:12–13). Increased agricultural productivity has been highlighted as a way to create employment opportunities and income among the rural population as well as lessen food insecurity (World Bank 2010).

Among Liberian youths, the agricultural sector is the dominant employer today. 33 per cent of the young work in fishery or agriculture (de Mel, Elder et al. 2013:2, 26). The youth themselves, however, do not seem to be interested in working within the agricultural sector. This was for example illustrated by the

---

8. "Informal non-agricultural employment and employment in agriculture accounts for 84 percent of total employment" (ILO 2009:10).

DDRR process after the second civil war and the packages ex-combatants chose. The most popular skills opted for were vocational training (50 percent) and formal education (42 percent) whereas agriculture was only chosen by 4 percent of the participants (UNDP/JIU 2005 in Munive Rincon 2010:120–121). Similar numbers were found among demobilised Liberian combatants at the end of the first civil war in 1997. Most of these fighters were between 15–28 years old at the time and when asked what they wanted to do after demobilisation 6 percent answered that they wanted to pursue farming whereas 56 percent wanted to go back to school and 28 percent learn a trade (Ellis 2007:132, see also Utas 2005b).

Instead, life in the city is perceived as providing future prospects and life chances. Many ex-combatants have for example chosen to remain in the urban areas, in some cases since they were afraid of the consequences of returning after their participation in the civil wars, in others they stayed to contribute to their families in the countryside through remittances (Munive Rincon 2010:27). Today, close to 70 percent of the Liberian population resides in urban areas (World Bank 2010:3). However, the jobs offered to ex-combatants and youths in the city are often low paid and insecure and the informal market is dominating.

Informal jobs are not regarded as proper jobs among young Liberians. Instead, youth dream of becoming formally employed; at an office, an NGO or perhaps for the government or within the UN (Munive Rincon 2010:230–232). Formal employment can however primarily be found in businesses related to the dominating export commodities like rubber, which represented 80 percent of Liberia's total exports in 2008 (ILO, 2009:10). Since waged employment, as mentioned in the previous section, is often found outside of the urban areas, youth and ex-combatants, have to leave the urban areas in periods to earn money.

Urban life is also connected to the appeal of modernity. In Liberia, modernity is a concept connected to consumption, technology, Western ideals and beliefs. Modernity gives youth a higher status in relation to the power traditionally vested in the elderly (Utas 2003:43–44).[9] Living and working in the big cities can arguably provide this. For now, many Liberian youth remain in the city and await paid jobs, according to the logic of the city as barracks (Hoffman 2007).

Migration, remittances and disputes over land

In Liberia, there has been vast internal migration as a result of the civil wars. During and after the wars there was also widespread migration of neighbor-

---

9.   A similar perception of modernity, "Western ideals" and urban life can also be observed in the Americo-Liberian settlers' aversion to agriculture in marking their belonging to a more "modern" or "civilised society" (see the first part of the historical section). See also footnote 7 on young Americo-Liberian women being economically dependent on their husbands.

ing countries. Many migrants have still not returned to Liberia and work and live abroad, in the EU or the US for example, and contribute to the economy through remittances. Remittances play an increasingly important role in the Liberian economy. Over the period of "January to November 2008, recorded inflows of remittances totalled US$ 884 million – an amount approximately equal to the country's estimated GDP" (ILO 2009:45). The argument could probably be made that for youth, similar perceptions of future and modernity that draw them to the big cities, could also make them look for a different life abroad. As described in the previous and historical section, those who migrate, whether it is to the city or abroad, make important economic contributions both to their family members and the country as a whole (see Utas 2010:116–118).

Another effect of the migration during and after the civil wars is land disputes. When IDPs and refugees return to find their land occupied, conflicts often arise. IDPs, refugees and ex-combatants are all looking for land and squatters in abandoned property are common. In some counties like Nimba and Lofa, ex-combatants have taken over empty properties. These disputes over land and property could perhaps lead to renewed outbreaks of violence (Bøås and Dunn, 2013: 47–50). Given the history of land being given to the Americo-Liberian elite or to international companies for plantations and extraction of natural resources, many grievances might lurk in the background.

Conclusion

The Liberian labour market has to a large extent, both historically and today, been dominated by informality. Employment possibilities and labour mobilisation have been, and still are, marked and shaped by patrimonial structures. The complexity of the (informal) labour market further emerges when taking into consideration the informality of the state (or more or less shadowy structures) – including a history of autocratic presidents with loyal patronage networks, the Americo-Liberian dominance, and the involvement of foreign business interests. The state has in many ways failed to deliver basic services and security to its people. History illustrates, however, that Liberia was never a state in Westphalian terms. As is the case in many other countries, the Western state format was imposed on Liberia with little regard to the indigenous populations and local governance structures. On the other hand, these local governance structures – the Wealth-in-People system or Big Men networks – have survived and continue to operate in parallel to, or in the absence of, the official state. On the individual level, the system of relying on big men (women) for the provision of jobs and security also stands in for the state where there is no official welfare system providing this. This duality, or perhaps plurality, needs to be taken into account when considering the structure of the Liberian labour market and how labour is being mobilised.

Youth could be mobilised into violent conflict but they are also the main actors for Liberia's future. Emphasising a potential for violence gives the issue of youth unemployment greater importance but misses the point and risks singling out this group as the alien other. Potential for violence has arguably more to do with inequalities and societal marginalisation rather than someone being young according to an age bound definition. However, it could be argued that the vast informal labour market in Liberia today, and the fact that much work is still contract based and short-term as well as low paid, hinders youth from becoming social adults and participating in society[10].

Absorbing unemployed youth into the military was historically a way for the government to impose control and consolidate the state. Working together with ex-commanders in the provision and distribution of peaceful labour opportunities today, as some researchers have suggested, has perhaps been an effective way of assuring integration of ex-combatants into society, as well as stability. Today however, in a society which is moving away from a militarised context, these

---

10. This paper has focused on unemployment and societal marginalisation in relation to violent conflict. Unemployment and marginalisation generate other types of violence as well, including gang violence and crime, but also domestic violence (more on these aspects, see for example Freeman 1991, Bourgois 2003, Krishnan, Rocca et al. 2010).

types of informal, Big Men networks are generally mixed, and consist of family, friends and colleagues.

When asking what jobs youth want, the answer is that they dream of formal employment. How can this be created? How can the informal networks that are so entrenched in Liberian society today be used in the best way? Is the resource extraction economy and agriculture the way forward, or how can work possibilities in the cities and in the formal state bureaucracy, as well as long-lasting employment opportunities, be created? What role do remittances play, particularly in relation to the division between the urban and the rural? What is the effect of an historical as well as contemporary unequal land distribution and the involvement of foreign actors in owning land and industries? These questions, including further mapping of the contemporary labour market and the Wealth-in-People system, are important to consider in future research relating to labour in Liberia. Finally, young women are underrepresented in current research as well as on the labour market. The structure of informal networks on the labour market in relation to young women would be interesting to explore further, and also "Big Womanity" and female strategies for finding work.[11] Another interesting aspect to look into would be labour unions as they can serve as important, and more peaceful, tools to air disagreements and grievances (see Cramer 2010:17).[12] The link between education, higher education and unemployment should also be further explored (more on this, see De Mel, Elder et al. 2013).

Unemployed youth are not prone to violence by definition, but they need jobs. Creating more employment opportunities is good both for the state and for its citizens. Understandably this is of high priority for Liberia and hopefully this paper has generated a more comprehensive and historically grounded understanding of the Liberian labour market. Hopefully, it can form the backdrop to future research on the topic of labour, employment and youth in Liberia.

---

11. Today, similarly to the historical section, young Liberian women are predominantly working as service workers or in shops and markets (46.4 percent). They are also found in agricultural work (30.4 percent) (de Mel, Elder et al. 2013:26).

12. According to recent estimates, less than a third of the working youth in Liberia are part of unions or worker's associations. See de Mel, Elder et al. 2013:34.

References

Abbink, J. and I. v. Kessel (2005). *Vanguard or vandals: youth, politics, and conflict in Africa*. Leiden, Brill.

Abramowitz, S. and M. H. Moran (2012). "International Human Rights, Gender-Based Violence, and Local Discourses of Abuse in Postconflict Liberia: A Problem of "Culture"?" *African Studies Review* 55(02): 119–146.

Akingbade, H. O. (1997). "The Liberian problem of forced labor 1926–1940." *Africa: rivista trimestrale di studi e documentazione* 52(2): 261–273.

Akingbade, H. (1994) "The Pacification of the Liberian Hinterland." The Journal of Negro History, 79(3): 277–296.

Akpan, M. B. (1973). "Black Imperialism: Americo-Liberian Rule over the African Peoples of Liberia, 1841–1964." *Canadian Journal of African Studies / Revue Canadienne des Études Africaines* 7(2): 217–236.

Azevedo, W. L. (1969). "A Tribal Reaction to Nationalism (part 2)." *Liberian Studies Journal* II(1): 43–63.

Bledsoe, C. (1990). "'No Success Without Struggle': Social Mobility and Hardship for Foster Children in Sierra Leone." *Man* 25(1): 70–88.

Bledsoe, C. H. (1980). *Women and marriage in Kpelle society*. Stanford, Calif., Stanford University Press.

Bourgois, P. I. (2003). *In search of respect: selling crack in El Barrio*. Cambridge, Cambridge University Press.

Bøås, M. and K. C. Dunn (2013). *Politics of origin in Africa: autochthony, citizenship and conflict*. London, Zed.

Collier, P. (2000). Doing Well out of War: an Economic Perspective. *Greed and grievance: economic agendas in civil wars*. M. Berdal and D. Malone. Boulder, Colo., L. Rienner

Collier, P. and A. Hoeffler (2004). "Greed and Grievance in Civil War." *Oxford Economic Papers* 56(4): 563–595.

Collier, P. e. a. (2003). *Breaking the conflict trap: civil war and development policy*. Washington, DC: World Bank.

Coulter, C., M. Persson and M. Utas (2008). *Young female fighters in African wars: conflict and its consequences*. Uppsala, Nordiska Afrikainstitutet.

Cramer, C. (2010). Unemployment and Participation in Violence. *Background paper for the world development report 2011*. Washington D.C., The Worldbank.

Cramer, C. (2008) From waging war to waging peace: Labour and labor markets. *Whose Peace? Critical Perspectives on the Political Economy of Peacebuilding*. Pugh, M, Cooper, N & Turner, M. Palgrave, London, pp 121–138.

de Mel, S., S. Elder and M. Vansteenkiste (2013). Labour market transitions of young women and men in Liberia. *Work4Youth Publication Series No. 3*. Geneva, International Labour Office.

Ellis, Stephen (2007). *The mask of anarchy: the destruction of Liberia and the religious dimension of an African civil war*. New York: New York University Press.

Eriksson Skoog, G. (2009). *Internal Concept Paper – Economic Development – towards a Strategic Focus*. Sida/Team Liberia.

Freeman, R. B. (1991). *Crime and the employment of disadvantaged youths*. Cambridge, Mass:NBER.

Government of Liberia (2005). National Youth Policy for Liberia.

Handwerker, W. P. (1974). "Changing Household Organization in the Origins of Market Places in Liberia." *Economic Development and Cultural Change* 22(2): 229–248.

Handwerker, W. P. (1980). "Market Places, Travelling Traders, and Shops: Commercial Structural Variation in the Liberian Interior Prior to 1940." *African Economic History*(9): 3–26.

Hoffman, D. (2007). "The City as Barracks: Freetown, Monrovia, and the Organization of Violence in Postcolonial African Cities." *Cultural Anthropology* 22(3): 400–428.

Hoffman, D. (2011a). *The war machines: young men and violence in Sierra Leone and Liberia*. Durham, N.C., Duke University Press.

Hoffman, D. (2011b). "Violence, Just in Time: War and Work in Contemporary West Africa." *Cultural Anthropology* 26(1): 34–57.

Honwana, A. and F. d. Boeck (2005). *Makers and breakers: children and youth in postcolonial Africa*. Oxford, James Currey.

Huntington, S. P. (1996). *The clash of civilizations and the remaking of world order*. New York, Simon & Schuster.

International Labor Organization (ILO) (2009). A Rapid Assessment of the Global Economic Crisis on Liberia. Geneva, Internatioanl Labor Organization.

Johnsson Sirleaf, E. (2006). Speech at the 95th International Labor Conference. Geneva.

Knoll, A. J. (1991). "Firestone's Labor Policy, 1924–1939." *Liberian Studies Journal* XVI(2): 43–75.

Krishnan, S., C. H. Rocca, A. E. Hubbard, K. Subbiah, J. Edmeades and N. S. Padian (2010). "Do changes in spousal employment status lead to domestic violence? Insights from a prospective study in Bangalore, India." *Social Science & Medicine* 70(1): 136–143.

Liberia Institute of Statistics and Geo-Information Services (LISGIS) (2011). Liberia Labour Force Survey 2010.

Käihkö, I. (2014). "Once a combatant, always a combatant?" Retrieved 21 January 2014, from http://matsutas.wordpress. com/2014/01/07/once-a-combatant-always-a-combatant-by-ilmari-kaihko/

Levitt, Jeremy I. (2004). *The evolution of deadly conflict in Liberia: from "paternaltarianism" to state collapse*. Durham, N.C., Carolina Academic Press.

Liebenow, J. Gus (1969). *Liberia: the evolution of privilege.* Ithaca

McEvoy-Levy, S. (2006). *Troublemakers or peacemakers?: youth and post-accord peace building.* Notre Dame, Ind., University of Notre Dame Press.

Moran, M. H. (2006). *Liberia: the violence of democracy.* Philadelphia, University of Pennsylvania Press.

Moran, M. (2012). "Our Mothers Have Spoken: Synthesizing Old and New Forms of Women's Political Authority in Liberia." *Journal of International Women's Studies* 13(4): 51–66.

Munive Rincon, J. (2010). *Questioning Ex-Combatant Reintegration in Liberia – Armed Mobilization, Localized Histories of Conflict and the Power of Labels.* Copenhagen, Danish Institute for International Studies.

Munive, J. (2011). "A Political Economic History of the Liberian State, Forced Labour and Armed Mobilization." *Journal of Agrarian Change* 11(3): 357–376.

Murphy, W. P. (2003). "Military Patrimonialism and Child Soldier Clientalism in the Liberian and Sierra Leonean Civil Wars." *African Studies Review* 46(2): 61–87.

Mynster Christensen, M. (2013). *Shadow Soldiering – Mobilisation, Militarisation andd the Politics of Global Security in Sierra Leone.* Copenhagen, Department of Anthropology, University of Copenhagen.

Pugel, J. (2007). What the Fighters Say: A Survey of Ex-combatants in Liberia, February – March 2006, United Nations Development Programme.

Reno, W. (2000). Shadow States and the Political Economy of Civil Wars. *Greed and grievance : economic agendas in civil wars.* M. Berdal and D. Malone. Boulder, Colo., L. Rienner.

Richards, P. (1995). Rebellion in Liberia and Sierra Leone: A Crisis of Youth? *Conflict in Africa.* O. Furley. London, Tauris Academic Studies.

Sawyer, A. (2005). *Beyond plunder: toward democratic governance in Liberia.* Boulder, Lynne Rienner.

Schulze, W. (1973). *A new geography of Liberia.* London, Longman.

Specht, I. (2006). Red Shoes : Experiences of Girl-Combatants in Liberia. Geneva, International Labour Office.

Themnér, A. (2013). Personal communication on field research in Bomi, Lofa and Montserrado, Liberia, during 2011–2012. E. Lindberg.

United Nations Development Programme (UNDP)/JIU (2005). "Reintegration Strategies – An overview of the implications of non-targeted assistance for demobilised ex-combatants". Reintegration Briefs No 3. Monrovia.

United Nations Development Programme (UNDP) (2013). "Rebuilding Livelihoods in Liberia." Retrieved 11 November 2013, 2013, from http://www.undp.org/content/undp/en/home/ourwork/crisispreventionandrecovery/projects_initiatives/rebuilding-livelihoods-in-liberia.html.

United Nations Security Council (UNSC) (2009). "Special Report of the Secretary-General on the United Nations Mission in Liberia."

Urdal, H. (2004). The Devil in the Demographics: The Effect of Youth Bulges on Domestic Armed Conflict, 1950–2000. *Social Development Papers*. Washington, DC, World Bank.

Utas, M. (2003). *Sweet battlefields: youth and the Liberian civil war*. Uppsala, Institutionen för kulturantropologi och etnologi, Uppsala University.

Utas, M. (2005a). Agency of Victims: Young Women in the Liberian Civil War. *Makers and breakers: children and youth in postcolonial* Africa. A. Honwana and F. d. Boeck. Oxford, James Currey.

Utas, M. (2005b). Building a future? The reintegration and re-marginalisation of youth in Liberia. *No peace, no war: an anthropology of contemporary armed conflicts*. P. Richards. Athens :, Ohio University Press.

Utas, M. (2008). Liberia Beyond the Blueprints: Poverty Reduction Strategy Papers, Big Men and Informal Networks. *FOI – NAI Lecture Series on African Security*, Nordic Africa Institute.

Utas, M. (2009). Malignant Organisms: continuities of state-run violence in rural Liberia. *Crisis of the state: war and social upheaval*. B. Kapferer and B. E. Bertelsen. New York, Berghahn books.

Utas, M. (2010). Abject Heroes: Marginalised youth, modernity and violent pathways of the Liberian Civil War. *Years of Conflict: Adolescence, Political Violence and Displacement*. J. Hart. New York, Berghan books.

Utas, M. (2012a). Introduction: Bigmanity and network governance in African conflicts. *African conflicts and informal power: big men and networks*. M. Utas. London, Zed Books.

Utas, M. (2012b). Urban youth and post-conflict Africa: On policy priorities. *NAI Policy Notes*, Nordic Africa Institute.

Utas, M. (2013a). "Generals for good? Do-good generals and the structural endurance of wartime networks." Retrieved 15 January 2014 from: http://matsutas.wordpress.com/2013/05/29/generals-for-good-do-good-generals-and-the-structural-endurance-of-wartime-networks/.

Utas, M. (2013b). "Once a General, always a General?" *Mats Utas* Retrieved 15 January 2014 from: http://matsutas.wordpress.com/2013/10/22/once-a-general-always-a-general/.

World Bank (2010). Liberia – Employment and pro-poor growth. Washington D.C., The Worldbank.

World Bank (2011). World Development Report 2011. Washington, DC, The Worldbank.

CURRENT AFRICAN ISSUES PUBLISHED BY THE INSTITUTE

Recent issues in the series are available electronically
for download free of charge www.nai.uu.se

1981

1. *South Africa, the West and the Frontline States. Report from a Seminar.*

2. Maja Naur, *Social and Organisational Change in Libya.*

3. *Peasants and Agricultural Production in Africa. A Nordic Research Seminar. Follow-up Reports and Discussions.*

1985

4. Ray Bush & S. Kibble, *Destabilisation in Southern Africa, an Overview.*

5. Bertil Egerö, *Mozambique and the Southern African Struggle for Liberation.*

1986

6. Carol B.Thompson, *Regional Economic Polic under Crisis Condition. Southern African Development.*

1989

7. Inge Tvedten, *The War in Angola, Internal Conditions for Peace and Recovery.*

8. Patrick Wilmot, *Nigeria's Southern Africa Policy 1960–1988.*

1990

9. Jonathan Baker, *Perestroika for Ethiopia: In Search of the End of the Rainbow?*

10. Horace Campbell, *The Siege of Cuito Cuanavale.*

1991

11. Maria Bongartz, *The Civil War in Somalia. Its genesis and dynamics.*

12. Shadrack B.O. Gutto, *Human and People's Rights in Africa. Myths, Realities and Prospects.*

13. Said Chikhi, Algeria. *From Mass Rebellion to Workers' Protest.*

14. Bertil Odén, *Namibia's Economic Links to South Africa.*

1992

15. Cervenka Zdenek, *African National Congress Meets Eastern Europe. A Dialogue on Common Experiences.*

1993

16. Diallo Garba, *Mauritania–The Other Apartheid?*

1994

17. Zdenek Cervenka and Colin Legum, *Can National Dialogue Break the Power of Terror in Burundi?*

18. Erik Nordberg and Uno Winblad, *Urban Environmental Health and Hygiene in Sub-Saharan Africa.*

1996

19. Chris Dunton and Mai Palmberg, *Human Rights and Homosexuality in Southern Africa.*

1998

20. Georges Nzongola-Ntalaja, *From Zaire to the Democratic Republic of the Congo.*

1999

21. Filip Reyntjens, *Talking or Fighting? Political Evolution in Rwanda and Burundi, 1998–1999.*

22. Herbert Weiss, *War and Peace in the Democratic Republic of the Congo.*

2000

23. Filip Reyntjens, *Small States in an Unstable Region – Rwanda and Burundi, 1999–2000.*

2001

24. Filip Reyntjens, *Again at the Crossroads: Rwanda and Burundi, 2000–2001.*

25. Henning Melber, *The New African Initiative and the African Union. A Preliminary Assessment and Documentation.*

2003

26. Dahilon Yassin Mohamoda, *Nile Basin Cooperation. A Review of the Literature.*

2004

27. Henning Melber (ed.), *Media, Public Discourse and Political Contestation in Zimbabwe.*

28. Georges Nzongola-Ntalaja, *From Zaire to the Democratic Republic of the Congo.* (Second and Revised Edition)

2005

29. Henning Melber (ed.), *Trade, Development, Cooperation – What Future for Africa?*

30. Kaniye S.A. Ebeku, *The Succession of Faure Gnassingbe to the Togolese Presidency – An International Law Perspective.*

31. J.V. Lazarus, C. Christiansen, L. Rosendal Østergaard, L.A. Richey, Models for Life – Advancing antiretroviral therapy in sub-Saharan Africa.

2006

32. Charles Manga Fombad & Zein Kebonang, *AU, NEPAD and the APRM – Democratisation Efforts Explored.* (Ed. H. Melber.)

33. P.P. Leite, C. Olsson, M. Schöldtz, T. Shelley, P. Wrange, H. Corell and K. Scheele, *The Western Sahara Conflict – The Role of Natural Resources in Decolonization.* (Ed. Claes Olsson)

2007

34. Jassey, Katja and Stella Nyanzi, *How to Be a "Proper" Woman in the Times of HIV and AIDS.*

35. M. Lee, H. Melber, S. Naidu and I. Taylor, *China in Africa.* (Compiled by Henning Melber)

36. Nathaniel King, *Conflict as Integration. Youth Aspiration to Personhood in the Teleology of Sierra Leone's 'Senseless War'.*

2008

37. Aderanti Adepoju, *Migration in sub-Saharan Africa.*

38. Bo Malmberg, *Demography and the development potential of sub-Saharan Africa.*

39. Johan Holmberg, *Natural resources in sub-Saharan Africa: Assets and vulnerabilities.*

40. Arne Bigsten and Dick Durevall, *The African economy and its role in the world economy.*

41. Fantu Cheru, *Africa's development in the 21st century: Reshaping the research agenda.*

2009

42. Dan Kuwali, *Persuasive Prevention. Towards a Principle for Implementing Article 4(h) and R2P by the African Union.*

43. Daniel Volman, *China, India, Russia and the United States. The Scramble for African Oil and the Militarization of the Continent.*

2010

44. Mats Hårsmar, *Understanding Poverty in Africa? A Navigation through Disputed Concepts, Data and Terrains.*

2011

45. Sam Maghimbi, Razack B. Lokina and Mathew A. Senga, *The Agrarian Question in Tanzania? A State of the Art Paper.*

46. William Minter, *African Migration, Global Inequalities, and Human Rights. Connecting the Dots.*

47. Musa Abutudu and Dauda Garuba, *Natural Resource Governance and EITI Implementation in Nigeria.*

48. Ilda Lindell, *Transnational Activism Networks and Gendered Gatekeeping. Negotiating Gender in an African Association of Informal Workers.*

2012

49. Terje Oestigaard, *Water Scarcity and Food Security along the Nile. Politics, population increase and climate change.*

50. David Ross Olanya, *From Global Land Grabbing for Biofuels to Acquisitions of AfricanWater for Commercial Agriculture.*

2013

51. Gessesse Dessie, *Favouring a Demonised Plant. Khat and Ethiopian smallholder enterprise.*

52. Boima Tucker, *Musical Violence. Gangsta Rap and Politics in Sierra Leone.*

53. David Nilsson, *Sweden-Norway at the Berlin Conference 1884–85. History, national identity-making and Sweden's relations with Africa.*

54. Pamela K. Mbabazi, *The Oil Industry in Uganda; A Blessing in Disquise or an all Too Familiar Curse? Paper presented at the Claude Ake Memorial Lecture.*

55. Måns Fellesson & Paula Mählck, *Academics on the Move. Mobility and Institutional Change in the Swedish Development Support to Research Capacity Buildiing in Mozambique.*

56. Clementina Amankwaah. *Election-Related Violence: The Case of Ghana.*

57. Farida Mahgoub. *Current Status of Agriculture and Future Challenges in Sudan.*

58. Emy Lindberg. *Youth and the Labour Market in Liberia – on history, state structures and spheres of informalities.*

www.ingramcontent.com/pod-product-compliance
Lightning Source LLC
Chambersburg PA
CBHW080210300326
41934CB00039B/3440